the COCKATOO and the GALAH

Neluta Kulic

IT WAS A BEAUTIFUL SUMMER MORNING AND A GREAT DAY TO PICK SOME RIPE FRUITS AND SEEDS FOR A DELICIOUS BREAKFAST. UP HIGH, ON A TOP BRANCH OF A FLAME TREE, WAS A BEAUTIFUL, SULPHUR CRESTED COCKATOO. WITH PURE WHITE FEATHERS AND A TINGE OF YELLOW ON THE UNDERSIDE OF HIS WINGS AND A YELLOW CREST, HE LOOKED MAGNIFICENT AGAINST THE RED FLOWERS OF THE TREE. THE COCKATOO WAS ENJOYING A JUICY BERRY WHEN HE HEARD A SOB IN THE DISTANCE. AT FIRST, HE DIDN'T PAY MUCH ATTENTION TO IT. AFTER ALL, HIS BREAKFAST WAS MORE IMPORTANT THAN ANYTHING ELSE.

HE KNEW THAT SOON ENOUGH, MANY OTHER BIRDS WOULD BE UP AND ABOUT SEARCHING FOR FOOD. IT'S NOT THAT HE DIDN'T WANT TO SHARE, IT'S JUST THAT HE WANTED THE RIPEST, JUICIEST FRUITS FOR HIMSELF. GROWING UP HE DIDN'T HAVE THAT PRIVILEGE. HIS PARENTS ABANDONED HIM AT A VERY YOUNG AGE DURING A CYCLONE. HE WAS TOO YOUNG AND TOO SCARED TO LEAVE THE NEST IN SEARCH OF FOOD SO HE ATE WHAT HE COULD FIND ON THE GROUND. HE ATE GRASS SEEDS, ROOTS, INSECTS AND BLOSSOMS BUT MANY TIMES, HE WENT TO SLEEP HUNGRY.

WHILE HE WAS TRYING TO GET A GUMNUT OPEN, HE HEARD THE SOB AGAIN. THIS TIME HE STOPPED AND LISTENED. THE SOB WAS COMING FROM SOMEWHERE NEAR, SO HE WENT ON SEARCHING. HE LOOKED UP HIGH IN THE TREES, HE SEARCHED DOWN LOW IN THE GRASS AND BUSHES, BUT HE COULDN'T SEE ANYTHING. SO, HE STOPPED AND LISTENED AGAIN... IT WAS COMING FROM A NEARBY TREE AND HE DECIDED TO FLY TOWARDS IT.

-4

HE LANDED ON THE TREE THAT HE THOUGHT THE SOUND WAS COMING FROM, HANGING ON TIGHT TO ONE OF THE TOP BRANCHES. AS HE WAS HANGING UPSIDE DOWN ON THE BRANCH, HE NOTICED A PINK GALAH.

"HELLO," THE COCKATOO SAID. "I AM SAM."

THE GALAH LOOKED UP AND STOPPED SOBBING JUST LONG ENOUGH TO RESPOND.

"HI! I AM FONZY."

"MAY I ASK WHY YOU ARE CRYING?" ASKED SAM.

FONZY REALLY WANTED TO TELL SAM THE TRUTH, BUT HE WAS TOO EMBARRASSED.

"COME ON, IT'S ALRIGHT," SAM INSISTED. "YOU CAN TELL ME."

"I LOST MY WAY," REPLIED FONZY. "I DON'T KNOW WHERE I AM."

"WELL, IF YOU TELL ME WHAT HAPPENED, MAYBE I CAN HELP," SAM OFFERED.

FONZY LET OUT A DEEP SIGH AND SAID; "YESTERDAY MORNING, MY BEST FRIEND ROSIE, TOOK ME OUT OF MY CAGE AND SAT ME ON HER SHOULDER WHILE SHE PICKED SOME FLOWERS FROM THE GARDEN. THE MORNING AIR WAS SO FRESH, THE SUN WAS SHINING, THE BIRDS WERE SINGING AND THE MORNING DEW WAS STILL ON THE GRASS. IT WAS ALL SO BEAUTIFUL AND PEACEFUL UNTIL A LOUD SCREECH FRIGHTENED ME AND I FOUND MYSELF FLYING. BY THE TIME I REALIZED WHAT HAD HAPPENED, I LANDED IN THIS TREE AND NOW I CAN'T FIND MY WAY BACK."

SAM WASN'T REALLY THE TYPE TO RUSH AND HELP ANYONE, BUT THIS LITTLE GUY SEEMED YOUNG AND FRIGHTENED. FONZY WAS SMALLER THAN SAM, WITH ROSE PINK FEATHERS ON HIS CHEEKS, THROAT AND BELLY AND PALE GREY FEATHERS ON HIS BACK, WINGS AND TAIL. HIS CROWN AND FOREHEAD WERE PINKISH WHITE.

"YOU POOR LITTLE THING, DON'T WORRY, I WILL HELP YOU FIND ROSIE. WE CAN LOOK TOGETHER," SAID SAM.

"THANK YOU, SAM, THANK YOU VERY MUCH!" REPLIED FONZY.

"LET'S SEE NOW, THE FIRST THING YOU HAVE TO TELL ME, IS WHAT DOES YOUR HOUSE LOOK LIKE? WHAT MAKES IT SPECIAL, UNIQUE, DIFFERENT FROM THE REST," SAID SAM.

"OH, DEAR ME," REPLIED FONZY. ALL I KNOW IS THAT IT HAS A BLACK ROOF AND A BEAUTIFUL GARDEN, FILLED WITH FLOWERS... AND A GUMNUT TREE... AND A WEEPING BOTTLEBRUSH BUSH. BETWEEN THE TREES IS MY CAGE. THAT IS ALL I REMEMBER. THIS IS THE FIRST TIME I HAVE SEEN MY HOUSE FROM UP HIGH. PLEASE SAM, YOU HAVE BEEN IN THESE AREAS BEFORE. DO YOU REMEMBER ANYTHING THAT SOUNDS FAMILIAR? DO YOU REMEMBER SEEING A BEAUTIFUL GARDEN AND A HOUSE WITH BLACK ROOF? DO YOU? I WANT TO GO HOME. PLEASE HELP ME."

IT IS TRUE THAT SAM DID A LOT OF TRAVELLING, ESPECIALLY DURING THE SUMMER MONTHS WHEN FOOD WAS SCARCE, BUT HE HAD NO REASON TO CHECK OUT THE NEIGHBOURHOOD. HE CAME THIS WAY A FEW TIMES, ON HIS WAY TO THE POND, WHERE HE WAS RAISED, BUT NEVER STOPPED TO CHAT UP ANYONE.

AFTER LISTENING CAREFULLY TO EVERYTHING FONZY SAID, HE THOUGHT FOR A WHILE...THERE WAS A HOUSE WITH FLOWERS IN THE GARDEN AND A BLACK ROOF, JUST TWO BLOCKS AWAY, BUT HE COULDN'T REMEMBER ANY TREES. THE BEST THING TO DO, WOULD BE TO GO AND HAVE A LOOK AROUND.

"OKAY FONZY, YOU STAY HERE AND I AM GOING TO SEARCH FOR YOUR HOUSE. IN THE MEANTIME, HAVE YOUR BREAKFAST AND I WILL BE BACK BEFORE YOU KNOW IT. I PROMISE."

SAM WANTED TO TAKE FONZY ALONG, BUT BEING MUCH YOUNGER, SAM DIDN'T WANT TO TIRE HIM OUT. HE WASN'T SURE HOW LONG IT WOULD TAKE TO FIND THE HOUSE OR EVEN IF HE COULD FIND IT, FOR THAT MATTER. AS HE WAS FLYING HIGH UP ABOVE THE TREE CROWNS, HE THOUGHT ABOUT FONZY AND THE HOUSE HE LIVED IN. HE WAS A LUCKY BIRD TO HAVE SOMEONE TAKE CARE OF HIM AND SHOW HIM LOVE. SAM WAS A WILD BIRD, NEVER HAD A HOME OR A HUMAN FRIEND. HIS CLOSEST FRIEND AND PROTECTOR WAS A DUCK HE GREW UP WITH. EVEN AS AN ADULT, HE DIDN'T HAVE MANY FRIENDS. SURE, HE KNEW A LOT OF PARROTS: JACK, THE YELLOW-TAILED BLACK COCKATOO, JOJO, THE GANG-GANG COCKATOO, TOMMY AND ZACK, THE LITTLE CORELLAS, BUT NO CLOSE FRIENDS. SAM WAS MORE OF A LONER. HE DIDN'T TRUST ANYONE. UNTIL HE MET FONZY, THAT IS. SO STRANGE THAT SOMEONE HE JUST MET COULD MAKE HIM CHANGE HIS WAYS.

SAM SHOOK HIS HEAD TO CLEAR HIS MIND AND GATHER HIS THOUGHTS AND TURNED HIS ATTENTION BACK TO FINDING THE HOUSE WITH BLACK ROOF AND A BOTTLEBRUSH BUSH. THE WIND PICKED UP A LITTLE AND SAM WAS THROWN AROUND A BIT, BUT KEPT GOING, USING ALL HIS STRENGTH TO STAY ON HIS PATH.

IT WAS VERY STRANGE FOR SAM TO BE FLYING AROUND AT THE NOON HOUR. USUALLY HE WOULD BE RESTING IN THE SHADE OF A TREE, CHEWING ON BARK TO PASS THE TIME. IT WAS VERY HOT OUTSIDE AND HE FELT A LITTLE SLUGGISH. HIS THOUGHTS WENT BACK TO LITTLE FONZY AND THE DANGERS HE COULD FACE IN THE WILD. SAM WASN'T WORRIED ABOUT BEING ATTACKED BY BIRDS OF PRAY. HE IS ONE OF THE BIGGEST PARROTS OUT THERE AND A VERY GOOD FLYER. BUT HE WAS WORRIED ABOUT FONZY THOUGH. PEREGRINE FALCONS LOVE LITTLE GALAHS FOR DINNER. SO DO THE GREY FALCON AND BLACK BREASTED BUZZARD. MAYBE THAT WAS ANOTHER REASON TO LEAVE HIM BEHIND. SAM WAS AWARE OF GALAHS SPEED AND FAST MOVES. DESPITE THE GALAH'S VULNERABILITY TO BIRDS OF PRAY, IN THE WILD, ITS FLIGHT IS STRONG AND RAPID WITH CONSTANT WING BEATS AND LITTLE RELIANCE UPON GLIDING. BUT FONZY WAS NOT A WILD BIRD. HE WAS SAFER IN THE TREE.

SAM SEARCHED AND SEARCHED BUT NO LUCK FINDING THE HOUSE. VERY DIS-APPOINTED, HE WAS READY TO TURN AND GO BACK, WHEN HE HEARD A CALL:

"FONZY, FONZY WHERE ARE YOU BOY?"

THAT MUST BE THE HOUSE, SAM THOUGHT. HE FOLLOWED THE SOUND OF THE VOICE THAT CALLED OUT TO FONZY.

"FONZY BOY, ARE YOU AROUND?"

THERE IT IS AGAIN. HE FLEW TOWARDS IT AND SAW THE HOUSE. SAM WAS ECSTATIC. "I FOUND IT! I F O U N D IT!" HE SHOUTED OUT LOUD. HE RESTED FOR A MINUTE ON TOP OF THE GUMTREE, THE ENTIRE TIME THINKING HOW HAPPY FONZY WOULD BE TO GET HOME. HE LOOKED AT ROSIE FOR A MOMENT. SHE WAS SMALL FOR A HUMAN, WITH LONG, BLACK HAIR, WEARING A COLORFUL DRESS. SHE WAS STILL CALLING OUT TO HIM, SEARCHING IN EVERY TREE ON AND AROUND HER YARD. HER VOICE WAS SOFT BUT THERE WAS SADNESS IN IT, AS WELL. IT WAS OBVIOUS

THAT ROSIE REALLY LOVED HER FRIEND AND SHE WAS DEVASTATED THAT HE WENT MISSING. SAM KNEW WHAT HE HAD TO DO.

WITH ALL HIS MIGHT HE TOOK FLIGHT AND HE DIDN'T STOP UNTIL HE REACHED THE TREE FONZY WAS WAITING IN.

" FONZY, ARE YOU THERE? I FOUND IT! I FOUND YOUR HOUSE! I FOUND ROSIE! LET'S GO, LET'S GO, I FOUND IT FONZY."

FILLED WITH JOY AND HAPPINESS, FONZY LET OUT A LOUD DOUBLE-SCREECH AND FOLLOWED SAM. THEY FLEW UP HIGH ABOVE TREES AND STREETS AND HOUSES UNTIL...

"SAM, THAT'S ROSIE, FONZY SHOUTED, AND SHE IS LOOKING FOR ME."

WITHOUT ANOTHER WORD, FONZY DESCENDED AND LANDED ON ROSIE'S SHOULDER.

"FONZY MY DARLING, YOU CAME BACK! I THOUGHT I WILL NEVER SEE YOU AGAIN, BUT YOU CAME BACK," SAID ROSIE. AND SHE KISSED HIM AND HUGGED HIM AND KISSED HIM AGAIN AND THEN SHE NOTICED SAM.

"I SEE YOU MADE A FRIEND," SAID ROSIE LOOKING LOVINGLY AT SAM. WHAT A BEAUTIFUL BIRD, SHE THOUGHT TO HERSELF.

"HELLO THERE. WON'T YOU STAY A WHILE. THERE IS PLENTY OF FOOD FOR BOTH OF YOU."

ROSIE LEFT THEM TO THEIR DINNER, WHILE SHE TENDED TO HER YARD. SHE WAS SO HAPPY TO HAVE HER FRIEND BACK. SHE TURNED AND LOOKED AT SAM. SHE GAVE HIM A SMILE AND SHE KNEW THAT FONZY MADE A FRIEND FOR LIFE. FONZY LOOKED AT SAM AND SAID;

"I THANK YOU FOR ALL YOUR HELP, SAM. I WOULD HAVE NEVER FOUND MY WAY HOME WITHOUT YOU. AND IF YOU WISH, YOU CAN STAY HERE WITH ME. ROSIE WOULDN'T MIND. SHE LOVES ME AND SHE WILL LOVE YOU JUST THE SAME."

SAM COULD FEEL THE LOVE BETWEEN ROSIE AND FONZY AND HE REALLY WANTED TO BE PART OF A FAMILY, TO HAVE SOMEONE TO LOVE HIM AND CARE FOR HIM. FONZY WAS A LUCKY LITTLE BIRD TO HAVE IT ALL.

SO SAM STAYED...

TELLWELL TALENT
WWW.TELLWELL.CA

ISBN
978-1-77370-679-5 (HARDCOVER)
978-1-77370-680-1 (PAPERBACK)